For

Thomas, Taylor, Charlie

Jack, Ben, Dean, Ashley

And the rest of my loving and supportive family and friends

Special thanks to my brilliant editor, Jennifer

© Alissa Powell 2022

Graphics by OlliArtDesign

Welcome to Animal Breathing Exercises for Children!

These exercises are designed for children ages 5 and up. Mindful breathing is valuable for all ages, but children often have trouble understanding the concept of diaphragmatic/belly breathing. Animal breathing is a great introduction to the power of breathwork, as the exercises are simple and the pictures are engaging.

Breathwork is a powerful tool that works quickly. Mindful breathing can calm an anxious child, safely allow them to express frustration or anger, and help them relax or fall asleep. The child may even perform better in school due to increased brain oxygenation, energy, and focus.

Animal Breathing is fun and easy to do with your children. Teach them the exercises when they are calm and happy, and practise the exercises until the child can do them. Then, when your child needs them, they will be ready. Ideally, the day will come when all you have to do is ask your child to do their dragon breathing, or do their bee breathing, and they will know exactly what to do.

See which exercises work best for your child. Have fun, be silly, and don't worry if they don't always get the exercises right. Children are more likely to use techniques they enjoy!

Happy breathing!
Alissa Powell, BBA, DipCNM, mBANT

Benefits of animal breathing exercises:

- Reduces stress and anxiety:
  Bee, Bird, Bunny, Dog, Snake, Whale

- Increases oxygen levels and energy:
  Bear, Bird, Dog, Dragon, Elephant, Lion, Snake, Whale

- Promotes calmness and relaxation:
  Bear, Bee, Bird, Cat, Mouse, Snake, Whale

- Releases tension, frustration, and anger:
  Dog, Dragon, Lion, Snake

- Improves focus and learning:
  Bee, Bird, Mouse, Whale

- Soothes emotions:
  Bunny, Mouse

CAN YOU BREATHE LIKE...

Pretend you are a bear just waking up from hibernation and you need to stretch and yawn a few times.

Sit cross-legged on the floor as you inhale through your nose and stretch your arms up to the sky.

Continue stretching your arms up, and then out to the sides and down to your lap as you exhale a big yawn through your mouth.

After a few times yawning, do your best bear growl as you exhale!

Benefits of Bear Breathing:
- Increases oxygen levels and energy
- Promotes calmness and relaxation

… A BEAR?

CAN YOU BREATHE LIKE...

Sit comfortably with your legs crossed and shoulders relaxed.

Stick your fingers in your ears.

Take a gentle, silent breath in through your nose.

With your mouth closed breathe out slowly through your nose making a deep humming sound in the back of your throat — like a bee — until you run out of air.

Repeat for a few minutes.

Benefits of Bee Breathing:
- Reduces stress and anxiety
- Promotes calmness and relaxation
- Improves focus and learning

... A BEE?

CAN YOU BREATHE LIKE...

Sitting either cross-legged or on your heels, start with your arms by your sides.

Breathe in slowly through your nose as you open your arms to the sides, spreading your wings horizontally.

Hold your breath as you soar above the mountains.

Breathe out through your nose as you bring your wings slowly back down to your sides.

Repeat.

Benefits of Bird Breathing:
- Reduces stress and anxiety
- Increases oxygen levels and energy
- Promotes calmness and relaxation
- Improves focus and learning

... A BIRD?

CAN YOU BREATHE LIKE...

Sit on your knees and heels and tuck your chin into your chest.

Get your nose ready for breathing by twitching it like a bunny smelling a flower.

Quickly sniff (take short breaths) 3 times through your nose, and then take a long exhale through your nose.

Repeat 5 to 10 times and try to increase the number of sniffs from 3 to 6 (or even 8!).

Benefits of Bunny Breathing:
- Reduces stress and anxiety
- Soothes emotions

... A BUNNY?

CAN YOU BREATHE LIKE...

Kneel on all fours.

Breathe in through your nose as you lift your chin and tilt your head back to look at the sky.

Breathe out through your nose while you slowly raise your back towards the ceiling and lower your head to look at your belly button.

Repeat.

Benefits of Cat Breathing:
- Promotes calmness and relaxation

... A CAT?

CAN YOU BREATHE LIKE...

Sit back on your heels and pretend you're a dog.

Take a gentle and quiet breath in through your nose.

As you breathe out, open your mouth, stick out your tongue, and pant like a dog (no inhaling, just exhaling) until you run out of air.

Repeat.

Benefits of Dog Breathing:
- Reduces stress and anxiety
- Increases oxygen levels and energy
- Releases tension, frustration, and anger

... A DOG?

CAN YOU BREATHE LIKE...

Sit on your knees and heels.

Sitting up tall, take a deep breath in through your nose. Exhale forcefully and completely through a big open mouth, whispering a roar. Try to make the exhale longer than the inhale. Be sure to completely run out of air.

Optionally, open your eyes wide and stick out your tongue as you breathe out your fire.

Repeat 3 or more times.

Benefits of Dragon Breathing:
- Increases oxygen levels and energy
- Releases tension, frustration, and anger

... A DRAGON?

CAN YOU BREATHE LIKE...

Stand with your feet wide apart.

Breathe in through your nose, raising both arms up with hands clasped together like an elephant's trunk.

Breathe out through your mouth while dropping your arms and swinging your hands through your legs.

Repeat 3 to 4 times.

Benefits of Elephant Breathing:
- Increases oxygen levels and energy

...AN ELEPHANT?

CAN YOU BREATHE LIKE...

Kneel on all fours, as if you were a lion.

Take a deep breath through your nose.

Open your mouth as big as you can, make a big scary face, eyes wide open...

And, ROAR!

Repeat.

Benefits of Lion Breathing:
- Increases oxygen levels and energy
- Releases tension, frustration, and anger

… A LION?

CAN YOU BREATHE LIKE...

Take small breaths in and out through your nose.

At first breathing may be fast.

Focus on gradually slowing down and keeping your breathing small and quiet – just like a mouse would breathe.

Relax your tummy and shoulders.

Breathe little mouse breaths for between 30 seconds and 2 minutes.

Benefits of Mouse Breathing:
- Promotes calmness and relaxation
- Improves focus and learning
- Soothes emotions

… A MOUSE?

CAN YOU BREATHE LIKE...

Sit comfortably with your legs crossed, shoulders relaxed and hands on your knees.

Breathe in through your nose for 3 seconds, hold for 1 second, and breathe out very slowly through your mouth while making a hissing sound like a snake.

You can move your body side to side like a snake as well.

Repeat 5 to 10 times.

Benefits of Snake Breathing:
- Reduces stress and anxiety
- Increases oxygen levels and energy
- Promotes calmness and relaxation
- Releases tension, frustration, and anger

... A SNAKE?

CAN YOU BREATHE LIKE...

Sit crossed legged on the floor.

Sitting up tall, breathe in through your nose and hold your breath like a whale swimming under water for 5-4-3-2-1.

Then look up at the sky and blow your air out through your blowhole (your mouth).

Repeat.

Benefits of Whale Breathing:
- Reduces stress and anxiety
- Increases oxygen levels and energy
- Promotes calmness and relaxation
- Improves focus and learning

... A WHALE?

About the author

Alissa Powell, BBA, DipCNM, mBANT
Founder of Breath Therapy™

Alissa teaches functional breathwork, pranayama, and mindfulness at her clinic in the UK, and online worldwide. She helps to optimise clients' physical and mental well-being by correcting dysfunctional breathing habits through breath retraining, Buteyko breathing, pranayama breath control, and other tools and techniques. She holds teaching qualifications from the Buteyko Breathing Association, Oxygen Advantage, and YogaLap.

Alissa is also a practicing certified Nutritional Therapist and gives breathwork talks and workshops around the United Kingdom.

BREATH THERAPY

Website: https://breath-therapy.uk

breaththerapy_uk/

BreathTherapyUK

Printed in Great Britain
by Amazon